SOUTH YORKSHIRE
FROM ABOVE

FLIGHTIMAGES

Photographs: IAN HAY, FLIGHT IMAGES

Text: MELVYN JONES

MYRIAD BOOKS

SHEFFIELD

From its origins as a medieval market town to an early industrial centre with its fame based on the water power of the river Don and its tributaries, Sheffield was transformed by steam power. As its steel industries expanded so did its population, which grew from just 40,000 in 1801 to more than half a million by 1921. It is now the fourth largest city in England. Since the dramatic decline of its light and heavy steel industries in the 1980s the city has transformed itself into a large post-industrial centre.

FROM HILLSBOROUGH TOWARDS GRENOSIDE

In every direction Sheffield's suburbs are graced with parks (described by one local writer as "pearls on a necklace") and woodlands (Sheffield is the best wooded city in the country). This photograph looks northwards over Hillsborough towards Wadsley Bridge, Parson Cross and Grenoside. In the middle ground is Hillsborough Stadium, home of Sheffield Wednesday football club. Lying to the south of the football ground is Hillsborough Park. In the background lie a number of the ancient woods for which Sheffield is well-known: Beeley Wood, Prior Royd, Wheata Wood and Greno Wood.

ACROSS THE CITY CENTRE NORTHWARDS

A close inspection of this photograph reveals a great deal of the history of the city. In the foreground is the so-called city spur, the rising ground south of the confluence of the rivers Don and Sheaf where the town of Sheffield was established in Norman times. The town grew southwards up the spur under the protection of its Norman lords and their castle to the parish church (now the cathedral) and beyond as far as the location of the modern town hall. The first modern extension to the early town took place in the late 18th century when the Duke of Norfolk, the major landowner, laid out an extension on a grid iron pattern still visible in the street pattern in the right foreground. Beyond the river Sheaf in the medieval period, in an area now occupied by the inter-war Manor housing estate and high-rise housing developments of the 1950s and 1960s, lay a deer park of 2,500 acres (1,000 ha). In the background lies the Lower Don valley that was transformed from a largely rural part of the parish of Sheffield in 1850 into an industrial area in the next 50 years by the expansion of heavy steelmaking.

CITYSCAPES

Right: Arundel Gate swings past the Central Library and Graves Art Gallery built between 1929 and 1934; the Lyceum, built in 1893 and completely refurbished in 1989-90; and the Crucible Theatre, venue for the World Snooker Championships. Behind can be seen the shop-lined High Street and Fargate, ending on the extreme left at the entrance to Orchard Square and the Town Hall tower. Halfway up High Street can be seen the white gleaming exterior of Kemsley House (the Sheffield Telegraph building) completed in 1916 and faced with faience. *Above:* the Canal Basin and its warehouses, renamed Victoria Quays, and containing a hotel, offices and an area for outdoor events. It was opened by the Prince of Wales in 1994. *Above right:* looking westwards along the city spur, up High Street and Church Street, over the Cathedral towards the University of Sheffield Arts Tower. Beyond are the suburbs of Netherthorpe, Walkley, Crookes and the middle Don valley. In the far background lie Stannington and Bradfield Moors.

LADY'S BRIDGE *(above)*

In the centre of the photograph is Lady's Bridge, a modern bridge across the river Don which hides below it a medieval stone bridge constructed in 1486. The bridge is named after the Chapel of Our Blessed Lady of the Bridge which stood to the south of the river. The builder of the medieval bridge, William Hyll, was instructed to "make a sufficient brigge over the watyr of Dune neghe the castell of Sheffield".

CONFLUENCE OF THE RIVER SHEAF AND THE RIVER DON *(below)*

The river Sheaf, which is now culverted in the city centre, runs from left to right along the bottom of the photograph. It was this river which gave Sheffield its name – treeless area beside the river Sheaf. At the junction of Sheaf Street and Commercial Street in the bottom left corner can be seen Pond's Forge International Sports Centre whose facilities include an Olympic standard competition pool, a leisure pool and fitness suites.

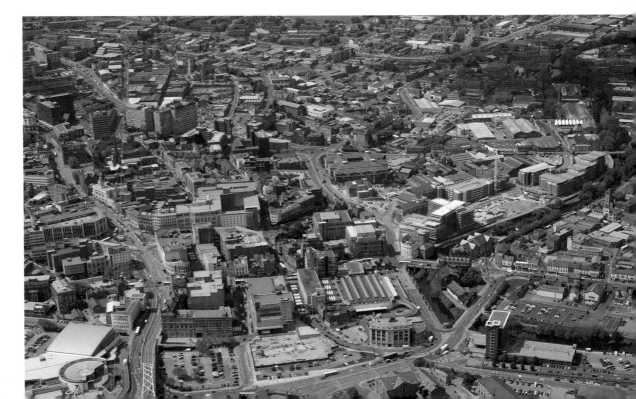

THE HEART OF THE CITY

The centre of Sheffield is dominated by the town hall, built of Derbyshire sandstone, standing at the junction of Surrey Street and Pinstone Street. It was described by Sir Nikolaus Pevsner as "a large picturesque pile". It was opened by Queen Victoria in 1897. Reflecting Sheffield's industrial history there are two friezes carved in stone around the exterior walls which depict, among other things, grinders, smiths, smelters and miners. The 200ft (61m) tower is surmounted by an 8ft (2m) high bronze statue of Vulcan, the Roman god of fire and furnaces. The £130m Heart of the City scheme has transformed this part of the city centre, with the opening of the Millennium Galleries, the Winter Garden, the re-designed Peace Gardens (originally developed on the site of St Paul's church, demolished in 1938) and a new hotel and office block (seen under construction here in 2004).

THE OLD MARKET AREA

(above)

The old market area of Sheffield lies in the bottom right-hand corner of the photograph. The medieval market grew up under the protection of the castle, whose site is still occupied by the Castle Market. The indoor and outdoor markets extended eventually to cover not only the castle site but also the surrounding streets as far as Haymarket, Waingate, Castlegate and Dixon Lane. Plans are currently afoot to relocate the remaining market hall from Castlegate to the Moor. Beyond the old market area can be seen Pond's Forge International Sports Centre, the Transport Interchange and Sheffield Hallam University.

THE BOTTOM OF THE MOOR *(right)*

This view shows the redbrick Department for Work and Pensions (originally the Manpower Services Commission) offices at the bottom of the Moor, with the Moor and Arundel Gate running to the city centre. Beside the roundabout on Bramall Lane can be seen St Mary's church built between 1826-30 and marking the southern extent of the pre-Victorian town.

PARK SQUARE *(above)*

This square (bottom right-hand corner of the photograph) is a major traffic focus that contains an important road roundabout that leads to and from Lady's Bridge and the northern entrance to the city; to Commercial Street for traffic entering the city centre; and to the Parkway leading to the M1 motorway. It also contains the bridges that carry the Supertram route from the city centre to Meadowhall.

THE ARENA *(left)*

This is a view from the south-east across the Lower Don valley towards Grenoside and Wharncliffe in the background. In the right middle ground is the Arena which holds 12,000 people and hosts international pop stars and is the home of Sheffield Steelers ice hockey team. Immediately to the left of the Arena is *iceSheffield* and further to the left with the tall poles over the entrance is the English Institute of Sport which provides state-of-the-art facilities and support services for world-class athletes.

THE ROYAL HALLAMSHIRE
HOSPITAL *(above)*

With its prominent 18-storey tower block, the Royal Hallamshire Hospital dominates the skyline for miles around. The plan for building this teaching hospital was approved in 1938, the architects were appointed in 1940, but then the war intervened and a start was not made until 1957. Beyond the hospital stands King Edward VII School, built originally as the Wesley College by William Flockton, the Sheffield architect, between 1837-40. In the top left-hand corner of the photograph, in the leafy suburb of Broomhall, can be seen various parts of the Collegiate site of Sheffield Hallam University.

HYDE PARK FLATS *(right)*

Gleaming in the sunshine are the re-clad two remaining tower blocks of the Hyde Park flats overlooking the confluence of the Don and Sheaf. Completed in 1966, the central block was demolished in 1992 and the two remaining blocks were taken back to their concrete frameworks and re-clad in red and yellow brick. Between the two re-clad tower blocks stands St John's church (1836-38) which originally stood among tightly-packed back-to-back houses.

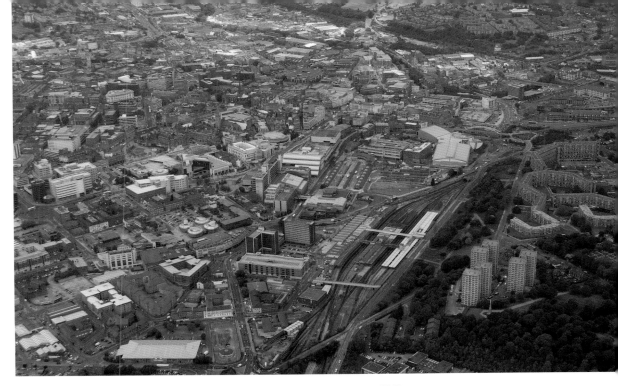

THE SHEAF AND LOWER DON VALLEYS *(above & below)*

The view above follows the Sheaf valley from the railway station to Burngreave in the background with the Park Hill Flats on the right. These flats, which were acclaimed by architects and sociologists in their early days, have also been referred to by other experts as extreme examples of 60s architectural brutalism. They are now Grade II (starred) listed and a refurbishment scheme has been agreed to transform the complex into upmarket apartments, rented flats and small business premises.

Sheffield did not get a direct railway route to London until 1870 when the station (then called the Midland Station) was built. Before that time a railway journey to London involved a trip to Rotherham on the Sheffield & Rotherham Railway, to board a train on the Midland Railway's line from York to London via Derby. Below is a panoramic view of Attercliffe in the Lower Don Valley with the Don Valley Stadium in the right foreground.

MEADOWHALL *(above, below and right)*

Dominating the eastern end of the Lower Don valley, beside the M1 motorway and on the site formerly occupied by Hadfield's steelworks is the giant Meadowhall Shopping Centre, a retail park with 1.2million square feet (116,000 sq m) of shopping space, 270 stores and free parking for 12,000 cars. Beside the shopping centre is the terminus of the Lower Don valley arm of the Supertram system, a mainline railway station and a bus interchange.

THE DON VALLEY STADIUM (above)

This industrial part of the city underwent significant change in the aftermath of the sudden decline of the heavy steel industry in the 1970s and early 1980s to become a much more diverse area. In the foreground can be seen the Don Valley Stadium, the largest athletics stadium in the UK, originally built for the World Student Games in 1991. Immediately to the left is the English Institute of Sport and beyond that on the left-hand edge of the photograph, is iceSheffield, which opened in 2003 and contains two Olympic-size ice rinks. Running behind the Don Valley Stadium and the English Institute of Sport can be seen the track of the Supertram, linking Meadowhall with the city centre. Beside Supertram on the left-hand edge of the photograph is the Arena concert venue. In the background can be seen the runway of Sheffield City Airport, opened in 1997 but which did not attract the volume of business that was hoped for and closed within a few years.

BRADFIELD MOORS *(right)*

About one-third of the area of the city of Sheffield lies within the Peak District National Park. It is difficult to imagine that just a few miles to the east is an urban area with a population of more than half a million. The upland pastures give way to coniferous plantations and heather moorlands, rising to nearly 1,800ft (548m). The reservoir shown here is the Dale Dyke Reservoir whose Victorian predecessor burst in 1864 causing physical destruction and human misery on a large scale.

THE LOWER DON VALLEY *(below)*

The river valleys around and in which Sheffield developed are full of contrasts. For 120 years the Lower Don Valley was the city's industrial heartland. Yet it was still predominantly rural until the middle of the 19th century. This had all changed by the beginning of the First World War. By that time Sheffield had become "the greatest armoury the world has ever seen". Most of that armoury was concentrated in the Lower Don valley. This powerhouse of industry was laid waste by the recession of the early 1980s when almost overnight 17,000 jobs were lost, firms with famous names went into liquidation and soon the valley was scarred by empty works, demolition sites and acres of rubble and twisted metal. In the last 20 years the valley has been transformed and now contains a mixture of premises old and new: steel plants, warehouses, offices, retailing parks, leisure centres and sports facilities.

THE LOXLEY VALLEY

In complete contrast to the Lower Don valley is the valley of the Loxley, a western tributary of the Don. The view is westwards along the valley from just beyond Malin Bridge with Loxley village occupying the slope to the north of the river and Damflask Reservoir in the background. The area beyond the settlement to the north of the river as far as Damflask Reservoir was once part of Loxley Chase or Loxley Firth, part of the private hunting forest (called Rivelin Chase) of the medieval lords of Hallamshire. The village of Loxley is one of the reputed birthplaces of the legendary Robin Hood, also known as Robin of Locksley. A survey of the Sheffield area in 1637 recorded "ye foundacion of an house or Cottage where Robin Hood was borne". In the woods beside the river to the south of the village can be seen the mill pond (called a dam in the Sheffield area)

of Wisewood Forge where four water-wheels were still in use as late as 1907. The Loxley valley above Malin Bridge is known to have contained 20 water-powered industrial sites. Just before midnight on 11 March 1864 this peaceful valley was the scene of one of Britain's major disasters. The Dale Dyke Reservoir collapsed and the waters of its reservoir burst down the Loxley valley towards Sheffield eight miles away. The crushing torrent of 114 million cubic feet (3.2m cu m) of water swept everything before it – cottages, farm buildings, water-powered mills, bridges, farm livestock and people. The waters swept on, unstoppable, down the Don valley into central Sheffield. 240 people were drowned, 415 houses and 106 works and shops were completely or partially destroyed, 693 farm animals were lost and 15 stone bridges were swept away.

BRAMALL LANE *(above and below)*

Lying immediately south of the city centre, Bramall Lane is the home of Sheffield United, nicknamed the "Blades". Bramall Lane was originally a cricket ground. Yorkshire County Cricket Club was founded in Sheffield in 1863 and county matches were played at Bramall Lane for more than a century. In its early days the ground hosted a variety of sporting events including athletics, cycling and even, in 1874, an exhibition baseball game. It became Sheffield United's football ground in 1889. This famous club were the Football League Division 1 Champions in 1897-98 only seven years after being elected to Division 2. Their record in the FA Cup is outstanding: they were winners in 1899, 1902, 1915 and 1925 and runners-up in 1901 and 1936. Harry Johnson has the honour of being the club's greatest goalscorer. In a career which began in 1919, he scored 250 goals in 342 appearances for United, including five cup goals on the way to Wembley in 1925. The record attendance at the ground occurred in 1936 at a cup-tie against Leeds United, when it was 68,287. The capacity of the modern all-seater stadium is 32,000.

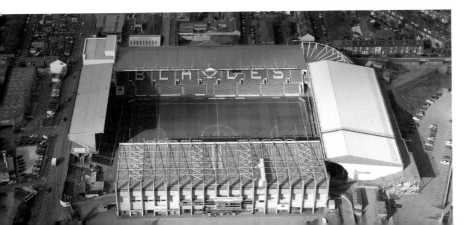

HILLSBOROUGH *(left & above)*

Located in north-west Sheffield, three miles from the city centre, Hillsborough is the home ground of Sheffield Wednesday – "The Owls". The club was founded in 1867 as the football side of Wednesday Cricket Club. After playing in different locations, Hillsborough became the club's ground in 1899, but did not take its modern name of Hillsborough until 1914. Wednesday have a fine league and cup record, being Division 1 champions in 1902-03, 1903-04, 1928-29 and 1929-30 and FA Cup winners in 1896, 1907 and 1935 and runners-up in 1890, 1966 and 1993. In 1961 a fine cantilever stand holding nearly 10,000 spectators was completed and in 1966 the ground staged a number of games in the World Cup. The record attendance at the ground was in 1934 when there was a crowd of nearly 73,000 at a cup-tie against Manchester City. The capacity of the present-day all-seater stadium is nearly 40,000.

BRODSWORTH HALL *(above)*

Besides the urban settlements, South Yorkshire has a rich heritage of country houses, parks, gardens and attractive villages and small towns. Brodsworth Hall, five miles north-west of Doncaster, is a fine Italianate-style country house, of Magnesian Limestone, built and furnished between 1861-63 for Charles Sabine Augustus Thellusson. The house and grounds remained in family ownership until 1990 when they were acquired by English Heritage. After a five-year programme of restoration and conservation they were opened to the public in 1996. Neat lawns surround the house which sits on a raised terrace of grass banks. Behind the house are croquet lawns and beyond them a large formal garden of symmetrical beds cut out of the turf in shapes said to have been unchanged since they were laid out in the 1860s.

TICKHILL *(below)*

Tickhill is one of the most attractive places in South Yorkshire. Despite the inevitable suburban expansion, the centre of the town still has the air of an ancient market town. Yet Tickhill did not grow naturally from an ancient village: it was an artificial foundation, a planned medieval town established by a Norman lord, Roger de Busli, to serve his estate and his main residence. The lord's castle was dominated by its motte, a hill 75ft (23m) high, clearly visible in the photograph, on which a timber and then an 11-sided stone keep was built. The new town built under the protection of the castle, was basically a one-street town extending up Castlegate to Northgate. Dominating the town today is St Mary's parish church, one of the outstanding Perpendicular churches of South Yorkshire.

WENTWORTH CASTLE *(below)*

Wentworth Castle is not a castle and not at Wentworth but at Stainborough. The hall consists of a north-west facing wing built by Sir Gervase Cutler between 1670-72 together with a north-east facing wing in the Baroque style which was finished in the 1720s and a Palladian-style front facing south-east built between 1759-64. The property was bought by Thomas Wentworth in 1708 and remained in the Wentworth and Vernon-Wentworth families until 1948 when the house, outbuildings and 60 acres (24ha) of garden were bought by Barnsley Education Committee. In 1949 it opened as a teacher-training college and in 1978 became Northern College. The grounds of the house hold a Grade 1 listing in the English Heritage Register of Parks and Gardens of special historic interest. It featured in the BBC Television's *Restoration* series.

WENTWORTH WOODHOUSE *(above & below)*

The magnificent Palladian-style mansion, Wentworth Woodhouse, was begun in 1732 by the 1st Marquis of Rockingham, and was still being completed by his son, the 2nd Marquis (who was prime minister twice) when he died in 1782. From that time until 1979 it was the home of the Earls Fitzwilliam. It has two distinguishing features. First, it was built on the back of a Baroque mansion which faces the other way; secondly, it has the longest front of any English country house at 606ft (185m). Running back from the front of the mansion can be seen the long walled terrace which forms the southern boundary of the wooded gardens. In front of the house is part of the large deer park which still contains a herd of about 100 red deer.

ROTHERHAM

These two views of Rotherham, from the west looking over the town towards Boston Castle and Park (right) and from the north over the town looking south to Clifton Park (above), show clearly the site and development of the town. Rotherham's origins lie close to an important crossing of the river Don, first as a ford and then as a bridge, below its confluence with the river Rother. The medieval bridge (which is clearly visible in the photograph to the right) still has one of only four surviving bridge chapels in the country. The chapel was built in the 15th century and travellers could give thanks for their safe arrival in the town or pray for a safe journey when leaving it. The town grew up on the eastern bank of the river Don where a low bluff gave a commanding position for All Saints' parish church (now Rotherham Minster). Before industrialisation Rotherham was a prosperous market town with its marketplace to the south-west of

the church. The compact early town grew up around the marketplace and church with extensions along Bridgegate, Westgate, Moorgate, Wellgate and Doncaster Gate. Industrial development began in the mid-18th century and was sustained throughout the 19th century. In its industrial heyday, manufacturing industry dominated the flat land beside the river Don, the importance of this industrial zone being greatly enhanced by the construction of canals (the New Cut, Brown's Cut and Rotherham Cut of the Sheffield & South Yorkshire Navigation) and railways (the Midland Railway in 1838 and the Great Central Railway in 1888). Now the scene on the flat valley floor is much more varied with retail outlets, a large superstore, a police headquarters and a bus station. At the top of the photograph above can be seen Clifton Park (which contains the recently renovated Clifton Park Museum) opened by the Prince of Wales in 1891.

CONTRASTING VIEWS OF ROTHERHAM

Left: looking from Centenary Way (running from left to right at the bottom of the photograph where it crosses the river Don) this view looks along Effingham Street to the minster and beyond to College Street, Moorgate Street and Westgate. This is the commercial and retail heart of the town. It contains the Central Library and Arts Centre, the market hall, bus station, Borough Council offices and the main shopping streets.

Below: in complete contrast is this view in Masbrough dominated by one of South Yorkshire's largest scrap yards, hemmed in (running in a clockwise direction) by the river Don and canal, the mainline railway between Rotherham and Sheffield, Masbrough Street and Centenary Way.

Trapped between the railway, Masbrough Street and the scrapyard is a green oasis formed by the green cut turf of Millmoor, home of Rotherham United Football Club, which came into existence in 1925, superseding two earlier clubs, Rotherham Town and Rotherham County. The record attendance at the ground is 25,170 in a game against Sheffield United in 1952. The modern ground capacity is 9,707. The club were Division 3 champions in 1950-51 and 1980-81 and Division 4 champions in 1988-89.

INDUSTRIAL ROTHERHAM

Industrial development began with the establishment of the Walker Brothers' Foundry in 1746. The iron founding tradition of the Walkers gave birth to Rotherham's important railway engineering industry, its stove grate industry and eventually to its steel industry. In its heyday heavy industry dominated the flat land beside the river Don from Tinsley in the south to Parkgate in the north. The products of Rotherham's iron and steelworks have been intimately connected to the nation's history: they provided the cannon for HMS Victory at Trafalgar, the plates that clad Brunel's Great Eastern steamship, shell steel for the artillery guns on the Western Front in the First World War and parts for the Mulberry harbours used at D-Day in the Second World War. Although there has been much decline in the iron and steel industry of the Rotherham area in the last 30 years, there are still about 21,000 workers (about 20 per cent of the borough's workforce) in the metal goods industry, although most are employed in the light and precision engineering sector rather than the heavy iron and steel trades. And industrial premises, if not the smoke and noise of previous years, still dominate the townscape as the photograph above and the two at the bottom of this page and the next page show. The photograph above is from the north across the industrialised Don valley, over the town centre towards Canklow and Canklow Wood. Even the wood is part of Rotherham's industrial heritage, having been managed for centuries as a coppice wood to provide charcoal for iron smelting. The photograph at the bottom of this page shows Corus Aldwarke Works where engineering steels are made and the photograph at the bottom of the next page shows the slag lagoon at the Aldwarke Works with the red glow of the molten slag.

MAGNA AT TEMPLEBOROUGH *(above)*

Templeborough Steelworks started production in 1917 as part of Steel, Peech & Tozer Ltd. In the 1960s Templeborough pioneered the production of carbon steel by electric arc melting and in the early 1980s it was the first British steel plant to produce engineering steels by the continuous casting process. The last cast of steel was produced on 25 November 1993. After standing empty for a number of years the steel melting shop of the former works, shown in the foreground above, was transformed into a hands-on science adventure centre called Magna. Here you can explore the four elements, Air, Earth, Fire and Water. Other major attractions are The Face of Steel, a multimedia show relating the history of the lives of local steelworkers and The Big Melt, another spectacular presentation bringing the electric arc furnace back to life.

CENTRAL BARNSLEY

(right, below and far top right)

For centuries Barnsley was a prosperous market town with a wire drawing industry. The original marketplace was on Market Hill but it gradually expanded to fill the whole of May Day Green. The town began to expand through the growth of linen manufacturing in the second half of the 18th century. By 1850 there were almost 4,000 handlooms working in the town in about 800 loomshops mostly in cellars, employing nearly 4,000 men, women and children. During the second half of the 19th century linen manufacturing began a long decline and by 1911 what had become a factory-based industry employed only 775 workers, mostly girls and women. The town, however, lay at the centre of one of Britain's most productive coalfields, which contained more than 20 productive coal seams including the world-famous Barnsley Seam, which attained a maximum thickness of 10-11 feet (around 3m). Coalmining replaced linen-making as the main employer of men and boys. At the height of its development there were more than 50 collieries on the outskirts of the town and in the surrounding mining villages. Now all the collieries have gone. And that is not the only change: the open-air market has also vanished to be replaced by an enclosed market hall. But one important building, erected when Barnsley was still the coal capital of South Yorkshire, still dominates the townscape and can be clearly seen on the photographs on the right and far top right – the Town Hall. Constructed in 1932-33, of white limestone blocks, it was designed by the Liverpool architects, Briggs & Thornely. It replaced the dingy old Town Hall in St Mary's Gate.

BARNSLEY BUS STATION (left)

Hemmed in between Eldon Street, Kendray Street, Queen's Road and the main railway line between Sheffield and Leeds, lies the revamped Barnsley bus station. Opened in November 1938, it was laid out and constructed by William Johnson and Son of Park Street Works, Wombwell. It had toilets, a café seating 100 and two newspaper kiosks, the one on the central island known affectionately as the "threepenny bit". For those with long and happy memories of travelling in from the suburban areas and from the surrounding mining villages to shop at the market, to buy their new Whitsuntide clothes at Barnsley British Co-op or to attend the Girls' High School or the Holgate Grammar School, this was the home of the Yorkshire Traction Bus Company – "t'Trackies". This company began life as the Barnsley & District Electric Tram Company in 1902. The first bus came into operation in 1912 and it started to cover a much wider area. Many readers will remember the continuous comings and goings of buses from the station to all parts of the surrounding area, all with the names of their destinations clearly displayed above the driver's window, including ones like "Jump Circular" that must have aroused incredulity and disbelief among newcomers to the area.

OAKWELL *(right)*

Oakwell is the home of Barnsley Football Club. Founded in 1887 by local clergyman Rev Tiverton Preedy, the club first played in the FA Cup in 1893-94 and entered the Football League (Division 2) in 1898-99. The club won the FA Cup in 1912. They won 1-0 after extra-time in a replay against West Bromwich Albion after a 0-0 draw. For one wonderful season in 1997-98 the club played in the Premier League when it was said that watching Barnsley was "almost like watching Brazil"! The re-designed and reconstructed ground now seats 23,000 spectators but in the old days when most of those attending a match stood for 90 minutes, crowds were much bigger, reaching an estimated 40,000 in a cup-tie against Blackpool who had Stanley Matthews in their side.

FROM PEEL STREET TO OAKWELL *(above)*

In the foreground of this panoramic view of Barnsley, Peel Street and Pitt Street run away to Peel Square. Many of the street names of central Barnsley reflect the rapid 19th-century growth of the town, for example, the names of prime ministers Peel and Pitt, other leading politicians like Eldon and Castlereagh and generals such as Wellington and Blucher. From Peel Square the eye travels left along Eldon Street and right along Queen Street, the junction marked by the distinctive white triangular building still partly occupied by Burton's the Tailors. Beyond Queen Street is Cheapside with the enclosed market hall occupying the site of the former open market area of May Day Green, and beyond that the Alhambra Centre. Beyond the Alhambra Centre lies the roundabout at the bottom of Sheffield Road leading on the left to Harborough Hill Road, a main exit road from the town towards Wakefield, the road crossing the main line railway line from Leeds to Sheffield. In the background, approached along streets of terrace houses, can be seen Oakwell Stadium.

MONCKTON COKE & CHEMICAL COMPANY *(above & left)*

Monckton Coke and Chemical Company continue a long tradition of coke-making on this site at Royston seven miles north-east of Barnsley town centre. Monckton Colliery, well located beside the then Midland Railway and the Barnsley Canal, started to produce coal at the end of the 1870s. In October 1879 the first beehive coke ovens came into operation and there were more than 150 coke ovens by 1890. By 1900 the coke ovens had the capacity to produce 1,800 tons of coke per week. The coal preparation plants were continuously modernised or replaced as the century progressed. Monckton Colliery was closed in December 1966. Today, more than 125 years after coke-making first started on the site, Monckton is one of Europe's foremost producers of metallurgical coke and smokeless fuels. Coke products are also supplied to chemical producers, blacksmiths and farriers; coke manufactured on the site is also used in brickmaking, soda ash manufacture, electrical earthing, roofing insulation and as a filtration medium.

DONCASTER (right & below)

The origins of Doncaster go back to Roman times, when a fort was established to guard the important river crossing of the river Don on the important military road from Lincoln to York. It grew as a market town in the medieval period and increasingly took advantage of its position on the Great North Road. It became an important industrial centre in the mid-19th century when the railway engineering industry was established. The Great Northern line had crossed the river Don near to the Roman crossing point in 1848 and in 1851 the decision was made by the Great Northern Railway Company to establish its permanent wagon and carriage repair shops in the town at Hexthorpe in a triangle of land between the railway and the river. The famous locomotives the *Mallard* and the *Flying Scotsman* were both designed and built there. The site can still be seen in the foreground of the photograph below. The town saw more growth after 1900 with the development of large, deep coalmines on the concealed coalfield that surrounds the town. Also prominent in both photographs is the tower of St George's church surrounded by trees in its churchyard. St George's was completed in 1858 to replace the medieval St Mary's that had been destroyed by fire.

Racegoers throng to Doncaster for the races, particularly the classic St Leger, which is run here each September. Doncaster Rovers is a well-known football club, while Doncaster Belles is one of England's most successful women's football clubs.

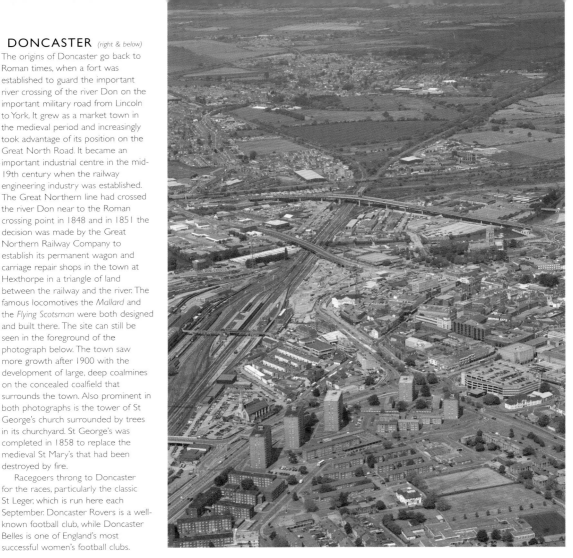

DONCASTER RACECOURSE *(above)*

Royal patronage brought horse-racing permanently to the town in the 17th century. The racecourse was established on the Town Moor. The racecourse is famous for staging in September each year the St Leger, the fifth and final classic of the British flat-racing season. The race was founded by Lieutenant Colonel Anthony St Leger in 1776.

CENTRAL DONCASTER *(right)*

The modern town centre of Doncaster has developed on and around its medieval nucleus with its many distinctive "gate" names, as in Baxter Gate, French Gate, Hall Gate and St Sepulchre Gate. This view shows the roundabout on Cleveland Street, with Trafford Way going right and left and Cleveland Street and Waterdale running towards High Street and Hall Gate.

CONISBROUGH CASTLE *(left & below)*

This is South Yorkshire's outstanding stone castle standing aloft on a tiny island of Magnesian Limestone and controlling an important crossing point on the river Don. It is one of the finest surviving pieces of early medieval architecture in England. The present castle began life as a timber motte and bailey castle in the years immediately after the Norman Conquest in 1066, built by William de Warenne who had fought beside King William at the Battle of Hastings. But Warenne was not the first to establish a fortification at Conisbrough. The name Conisbrough, which it is assumed predates the coming of the Normans, means "king's stronghold", but to which king this refers is not known. The massive cylindrical tower of the keep is 85ft (26m) high and its walls are up to 15ft (4.5m) thick. Restoration began in 1992 and the floors of the keep have been reinstated and its conical roof is once more in place.

In the background of the left-hand photograph can be seen crossing the river Don, the 1,527ft (465m) long, 21-arched viaduct of the Dearne Valley Railway completed at the beginning of the last century.

First published in 2009 by Myriad Books Limited
35 Bishopsthorpe Road, London SE26 4PA

Photographs © Ian Hay, Flight Images,
with the exception of those on pages 18-19,
which are © Peter Smith Photography
Text copyright © Melvyn Jones
Melvyn Jones has asserted his right under the
Copyright, Designs and Patents Act 1998 to be
identified as the author of this work.

ISBN 1 84746 235 9

Designed by Jerry Goldie
Printed in China

www.myriadbooks.com